D0565011

ADVENTURE TIME
VOLUME 2

kaboom!
CN
CARTOON NETWORK
FREDERATOR

ADVENTURE TIME Volume Two Scholastic Edition — February 2013. Published by KaBOOM!, a division of Boom Entertainment, Inc.

For information regarding the CPSIA on this printed material, call: (203) 595-3636 and provide reference #RICH – 464876. A catalog record of this book is available from OCLC and from the KaBOOM! website, www.kaboom-studios.com, on the Librarians Page.

BOOM! Studios, 5670 Wilshire Boulevard, Suite 450, Los Angeles, CA 90036-5679. Printed in USA. First Printing. ISBN: 978-1-60886-327-3

CREATED BY
Pendleton Ward

WRITTEN BY
Ryan North

ILLUSTRATED BY
Shelli Paroline and Braden Lamb

ADDITIONAL COLORS BY
Lisa Moore

"ADVENTURE TIM"

ILLUSTRATED BY
Mike Holmes

COLORS BY **STUDIO PARLAPÀ**

LETTERS BY
Steve Wands

COVER BY
Chris Houghton

COLORS BY **KASSANDRA HELLER**

EDITOR
Shannon Watters

ASSISTANT EDITOR
Adam Staffaroni

TRADE DESIGN
Stephanie Gonzaga

With special thanks to
Marisa Marionakis, Rick Blanco, Curtis Lelash, Laurie Halal-Ono, Keith Mack, Kelly Crews and the wonderful folks at Cartoon Network.

i hope i'm
GOOD AT THIS
EGGS
MILK
+
FLOUR

Finn! Jake!
Come quick!
ICING

I made BAKING!!

i hope i'm GOOD AT THIS

I wrote this page while eating baking. It was a singular moment of perfection.

BAKING!!
I LOVE EATING BAKING!!

No man, I love eating baking the most!
You can eat baking when I'm done eating baking!

Finn and Jake, there is no need to get stuck in the door! I made this "cup cake" for you to SHARE.
But it's kinda... tiny?

Jake, would you rather have half a "cup cake" or none of a "cup cake"?
I'm gonna order off-menu, BMO. One whole cupcake please!
i hope i'm GOOD AT THIS

Wait! I've got an AMAZING IDEA to figure out who gets to gobble the cupcake!
I love amazing ideas!
I know man, me too!

BMO, give us a challenge!! Then whoever completes the challenge best gets to eat the whole cupcake!
TOTAL MATH. But BMO, make the challenge "who can be the most Jake-like", okay?

I'm super terrific at that.

My editor insisted that the next scene be cut, so you'll just have to IMAGINE sixteen pages of Finn and Jake, still stuck in the doorway, talking about their feelings.

SOON:
On your mark!

Get set!
Wait, you haven't told us what the challenge is yet!

As you know, Finn and Jake, only he who defeats my ultimate challenge will be permitted to gobble my baking. And the challenge you must now face is...
i hope i'm

WHO CAN GO THE FURTHEST IN A STRAIGHT LINE??
GOOD AT THIS

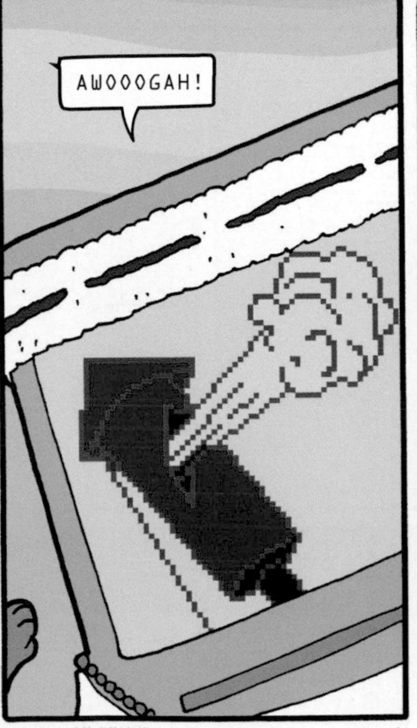
AWOOOGAH!

That was the whistle! GO, GO!!
GOOD AT THIS

FILE NOT FOUND: reasonable_whistle_sound.mp3

Good luck Finn and Jake!

Finally some time alone! Now I can continue building my creepy Finn and Jake robots!
GOOD AT THIS

Bro I love you but you're not going to go in a straighter line than me!
Bro that emotion is reciprocated but I am the best there is at what I do, and what I do is run in a really straight line!

Bro I think you're great but I can tell you're slowing down because running this fast is hard work!
Bro I'm really glad we're friends but you too are a'huffin and a'puffin!

Bro I look forward to years of friendship with you but what if we just walked for a bit.
Bro I cannot conceive of a future without you in it somewhere and yeah let's--let's do that.

That's not creepy enough!!

Where are we, dude? I've never been this far out before.
At least we can't get lost, since all we have to do is just turn around and walk backwards when we give up.
Wait, I mean when **YOU** give up!

Ha! You're gonna give up soon when you see how awesome I am at **NOT** giving up ever!
Ha! I'd like to see that! I mean I'd like to see the opposite, where I don't give up and get a cupcake because of it!!

That'll only happen if I share my cupcake winnings with you due to my **ULTIMATE BEST FRIEND GENEROSI--**
Hey, what's that up ahead?

So much for your straight line, brotime! Looks like **I'M** going to be eating a **DELICIOUS CAKE** from a **CUP**!

...Oh, right.

Well, you're just lucky that wall didn't go up infinity high.
I know it, dude!!

We're all lucky that wall didn't go up infinity high, because that'd take a really long time to draw, plus it would make this comic the longest thing in the universe!

Finn! Can you help me please?
I climbed into this clay bucket because I wanted to see if it was awesome to be inside one but it's not and now I'm **STUCK!**
Not a problem, Princess!!

So... close...!
Looks like **YOU'RE** gonna have to stop walking in a straight line to help her, dude!

Jake, can you save her real quick? You can totes do it without stepping out of line!
I want Finn to save me, please!
Sorry dude! Lady's choice!

Wait a sec, I can auto-tune my voice while singing! It's what I got when I leveled up after I swallowed that computer!
So?
So isn't Acoustics Princess always saying that if I sing loud enough at the right frequency, I can shatter any pot?

Lah lah lah lah laaaaaaaaaaa aaaaaa**AAAAAAAAAA**
Oh ha ha this is one of my favorite songs

AAAAAAAAAAAAH!
Yay, thanks Finn! Me and the lampreys I'm made out of owe you one!

Yes, Acoustics Princess! You mean you haven't...*HEARD* of her?

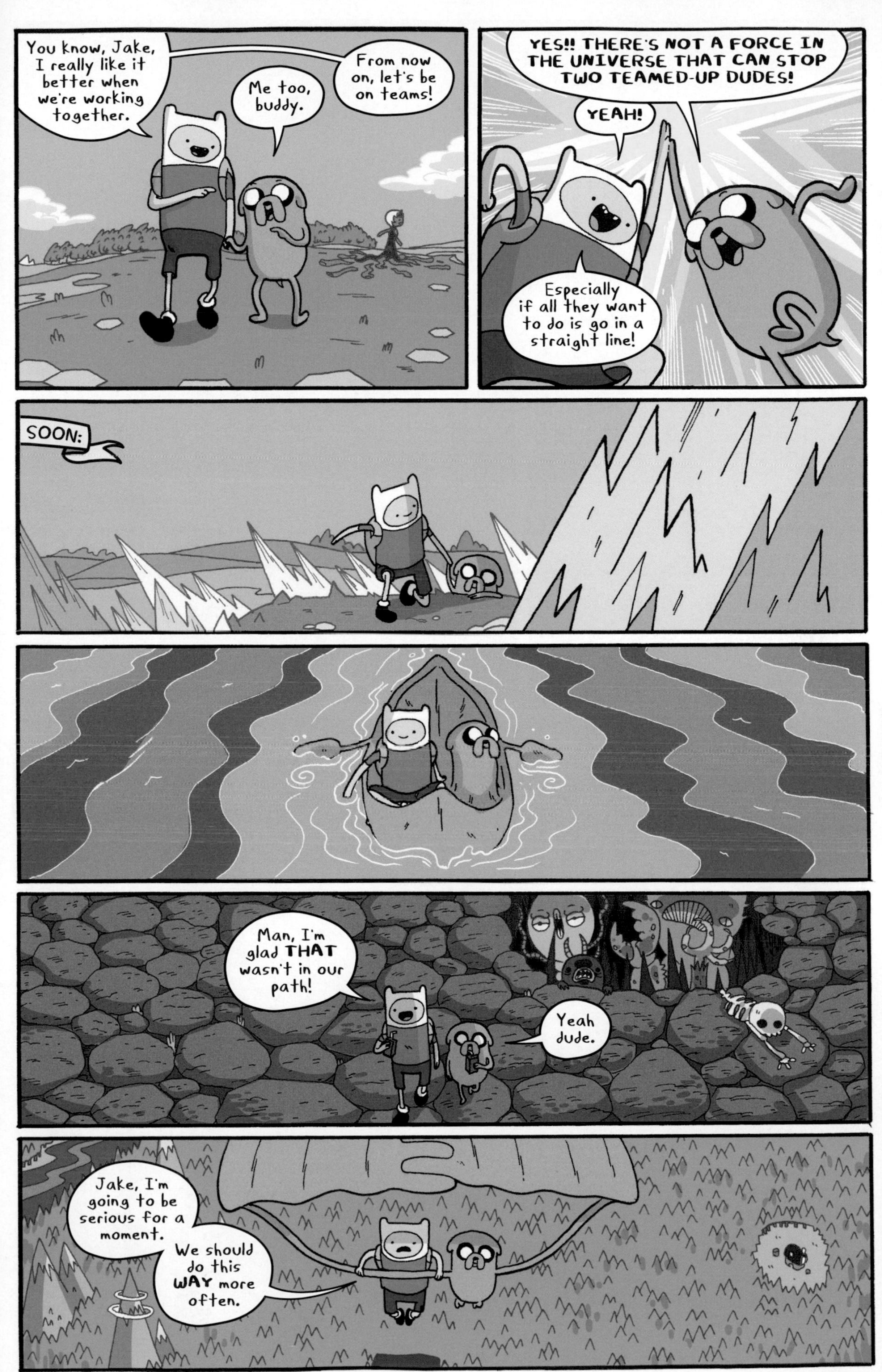
You know, Jake, I really like it better when we're working together.
Me too, buddy.
From now on, let's be on teams!
YES!! THERE'S NOT A FORCE IN THE UNIVERSE THAT CAN STOP TWO TEAMED-UP DUDES!
YEAH!
Especially if all they want to do is go in a straight line!
SOON:
Man, I'm glad THAT wasn't in our path!
Yeah dude.
Jake, I'm going to be serious for a moment.
We should do this WAY more often.

Aw man! This one blocks **BOTH** of us.
How are we gonna get past this one, Finn? I'd really prefer to do it in the laziest way possible.
NONE SHALL PASS

Hey, wait a second...

NOT A PROBLEM!!
* unless you can think of a bunch of things that rhyme with "butt"

"Gut"!!
"Strut"!

"Say what?"
"Peanut"!

NONE SHALL PASS
Hey, thanks guys! That's great!
That'll help my poetry writer's block for sure!!

'Twas brillig, and the slithy toves / Did gyre and gimble near the butt: All mimsy were the borogoves / And the mome raths were all, "say what?"

Whoa, Jake! Scope that tight tree fort!
Ti-yi-yight! But it's right in our way.
No problem! We'll knock on their door and ask if they mind two strangers walking through their house in a perfectly straight line!

It's a reasonable request. They probably get it all the time.
Dude, meeting someone new is totally an adventure! You know what that means!
WHAT TIME IS IT??

ADDDDVENTURE TIME!!
BUMP

Hey, I thought I heard someone here! Please, come in.
My name's Tim, and I love going on adventures. People call me...

Adventure Tim!!
BUMP

Please, come on in, and grab your friend! You've come from a very distant land, haven't you?

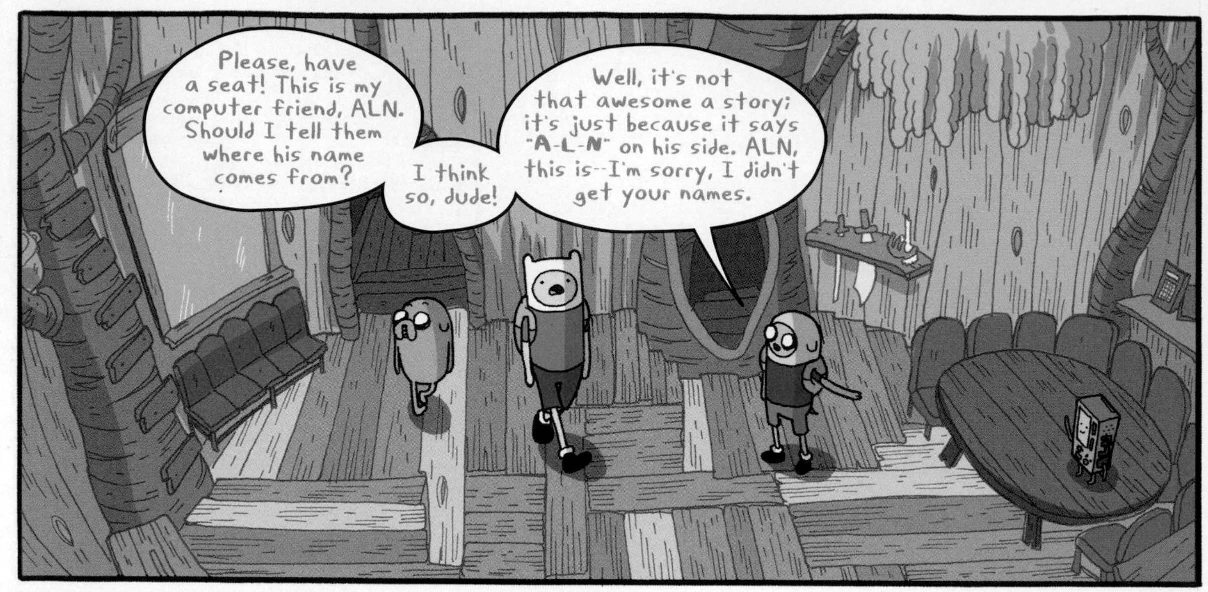
Please, have a seat! This is my computer friend, ALN. Should I tell them where his name comes from?
I think so, dude!
Well, it's not that awesome a story; it's just because it says "A-L-N" on his side. ALN, this is--I'm sorry, I didn't get your names.

Um, I'm Jake.
Wait! I mean, he's Jake!
And HE'S Finn!

Dude. Does he seem nutty to you?
Yeah man. It's like he's got two best friends up there in his head, and they take turns on the mouth controls!
Weiiiiird.

Finn and Jake, I would offer you a cup cake I baked all by myself, but Tim here gobbled the whole thing!
Hah! That's--that's okay!

Dude, he even has a robot pal who baked a tiny cake! And his action phrase is crazy close to what we say!
I know, man! I don't understand! Just--just be cool till we can figure this out, okay?

So, um, Tim... Tell me about yourself! What's your thing?
I fight evildoers for justice!
AND I save Princesses from the Mice King!
MICE King?!

Alternates considered here: Rice King, Lice King, Twice King (two heads), Price King (dollar signs for eyes), and Flotation Device King (his puffy body is a fun way to stay safe on the beach)

Interesting, interesting. And what princesses do you save?
Oh, tons. There's Princess Chewypaste, Irregular Topography Expanse Princess, Lunchbox Princess...
But I don't do it on my own!

Let me guess: you have help from Marhige the Vampire Liege?
No, I don't know that person. I do sometimes team up with Cinnamon Roll though!
Ooh! And Lady Unibow! She's the greatest.

I've heard enough! And now I want to flip this table while I say the following:
DUDE, STOP COPYING OUR LIVES!!

What do you mean, "copying"?
Come on, man! Mice King is a total knock-off of the Ice King!
Wait: ICE King?! So he lives inside the guts of a giant... ice cube?

And Princess Chewypaste sounds like a grosser version of Princess Bubblegum!
She's not gross, she's nice! She's made out of chewy paste.
THAT DOES ACTUALLY SOUND NICE, BUT STILL.

But look at you, man! You're like me and Finn all mixed together into one ultimate dude!
Not that that's a bad thing.
Okay yeah, that one part is pretty cool too.

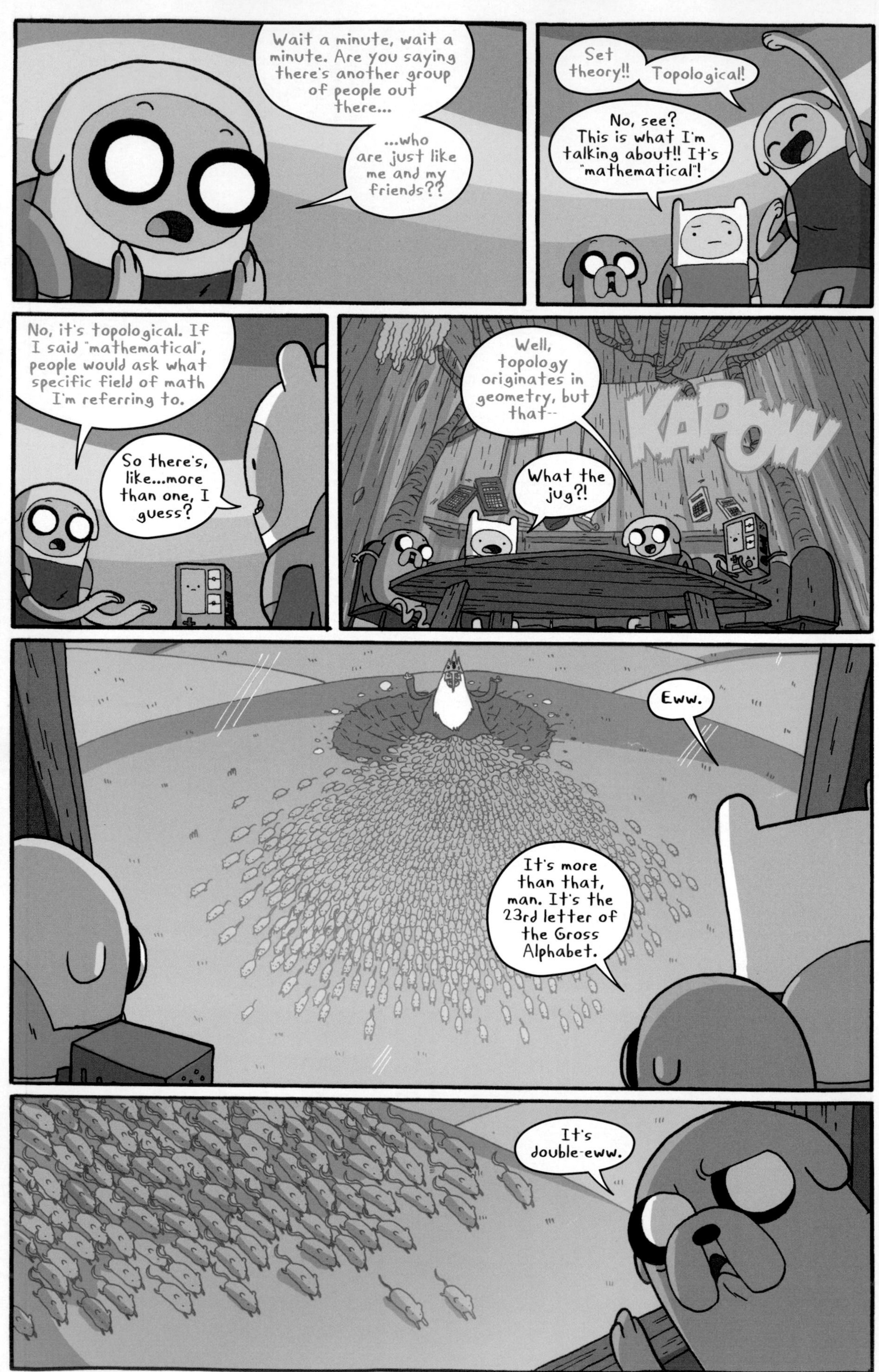

Wait a minute, wait a minute. Are you saying there's another group of people out there...
...who are just like me and my friends??
Set theory!!
Topological!
No, see? This is what I'm talking about!! It's "mathematical"!
No, it's topological. If I said "mathematical", people would ask what specific field of math I'm referring to.
So there's, like...more than one, I guess?
Well, topology originates in geometry, but that--
KAPOW
What the jug?!
Eww.
It's more than that, man. It's the 23rd letter of the Gross Alphabet.
It's double-eww.

The 16th letter is another highlight of the Gross Alphabet, though it's also shared with the Funny Alphabet and the Oh No What's In This Bottle Alphabet.

Mice King! What are you doing here?!
I came to see if your visitors were princesses! They looked like they might be princesses!
Why are you punching up my mice, Timberly?

BECAUSE YOU'RE EVIL!!
We're wicked good at fighting evil!
Wait, he's evil? Why didn't you say so?!

Hey, evil Mice King! Here's some punches for your lunches!!
What are you guys talking about? I'm not evil!
I'm more like...chaotic neutral!

Is this true, Tim?!
Not according to this chart!

See?
Lawful good PRINCESS CHEWYPASTE
Neutral good ADVENTURE TIM
LAWFUL NEUTRAL DUKE OF LIMESnatCH
TRUE NEUTRAL TOPIARY NOSE
LAWFUL evil mow-me
NEUTRAL EVIL mice KING
CHAOTIC EVIL THE LOCH
it's a kind of lake

"Neutral evil"?! I'll show you neutral evil!
Guntors! Attack everyone equally, even the new guys!

Finn, this is weird and gross. I don't like this one bit.
Me neither, man. Let's beat up the Mice King and get out of here.

Tim! It's time to put the Mice King to bed!!
Okay sure!!
No, Guntor, not me!! I didn't mean attack me!

Ready... aim...
FIRE!!

MICE to see you!!
BAM

You know what?
What?
I never realized how gross this is until now.
I hear you, man.

Tim lives for the day he's fighting alongside another guy named Tim, so that somebody might set him up with a perfectly-timed "Which Tim is it?"

Well, it was nice to meet you and all, but Jake and I are a little weirded out by all this.
Plus we stopped walking in a straight line way back there!
AW MAN, I FORGOT!!

Are you sure you can't stay? We were pretty great at team-ups!
Yeah man, our team was... "totally math".

Heh. Yeah it was, but we should really go.
Okay! Topographical or whatever!! See you later!

You know, those guys remind me of someone.

Huh.
Weeee!

Oh well! Come on, ALN. We've got to go get dinner ready for my hot date tonight!!
Weeee!

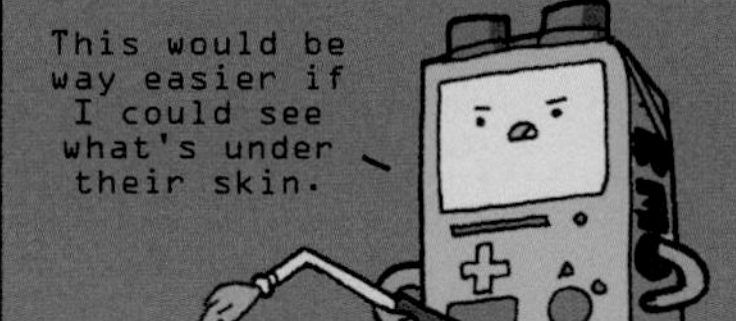
This would be way easier if I could see what's under their skin.

THAT EVENING:
BMO! BMO!
You won't believe it, BMO! WE MET A CRAZY DUDE!

Hello Finn! Hello Jake! Welcome home! You have -ONE- unheard message:

Hi guys! I came by to ask for help finishing my insane new invention, but BMO told me you were out on important business!
Sweet. Thanks BMO!

Unfortunately neither of you could stay within a 0.05mm variance of a straight line, so nobody won first place in my ultimate challenge!
Wait. How'd you know how we walked, BMO?
Finn
Jake

Every time you guys leave the house, I go up on the roof and watch everything you do through the telescope!

Then you saw the Adventure Tim? And the Mice King?
No, Finn! I got crazy bored and had a nap.
That whole thing was so crazy! Could it all have been, I dunno, a hallucination brought on by walking in a straight line for way too long??

I dunno, man. My shirt smells like stanky mice parts.
Oh Yeah. Bleh.

However, the second-place prize in my ultimate challenge is that we all share my baking together!
YAY!
Finn→
←Jake

Isn't it weird to think that Adventure Tim is out there, having similar but slightly different adventures every second of every day?
Yeah!

MEANWHILE, ELSEWHERE:
Isn't it weird to think that Finn and Jake are out there, having similar but slightly changed adventures all the time?
Yeah!

Wait! That means that **WE** can control his adventures by changing what we do!
Hah hah! **YES.** Check this out, dude!
Thhbbbpb-pbpbh!

MEANWHILE, ELSEWHERE:
Thhbbbpb-pbpbh!
Wait, wait! I don't know why I'm doing this!!

Heh heh heh.
THE END!

Finn! In the next issue we should totes find out what's up with Princess Bubblegum's invention!

Oh man! Totes!!

Attach the face to the body...
SCIENCE TABL

...attach two hands directly to the face...
...and...

YES! Finished!
I've finally created my greatest invention...

A TIME MACHINE.

Yep! It's an alarm clock! A machine that tells time!
Now I won't be late for appointments!

Oh, I guess this invention is pretty much done too...

1230
AN ACTUAL REAL-LIFE TIME MACHINE!!

Hey Princess! Whatcha got there?
Is it a machine?

Finn, Jake! You're just in time! Look what I made!
It looks like some kind of machine!
1230

It's a time machine, dudes.
Whoa! SERIOUSLY?
A TIME MACHINE??

Princess I need to borrow this! I need to go back in time and tell baby me how to be cool!
When I was a baby I wasn't nearly as cool as I am now!!

I did boom boom in my diapers, like, ALL THE TIME.

I know, bro.
I know.

We've all done boom boom in places we regret, buddy.

I didn't invent a time machine to stop you from being an uncool baby, Jake.
That's okay! I don't mind! We can still use it for that!

Actually, no, we can't. All my time machine does is let you go back to when I first invented it!
Aw man, really? That's only a few seconds ago! That stinks, Princess!

Oh, I'm sorry Jake! Is my **MACHINE THAT SENDS PEOPLE CAREENING THROUGH TIME** not impressive enough for you?
No no, it's pretty impressive. I **GUESS**.
Have you tried it out yet, Peebles?

Actually, I haven't. The first press of the button will require preparation, scientific controls and a coordinated cross-temporal team effort.
Teamwork?! Not a problem!

Wait, what are you doing?
There, we're a team!

And I'm pretty sure this is going to work!

It's okay, Princess Bubblegum... I'M impressed with your time machine. You've made way more progress on yours than I ever did!

90 SECONDS AGO:
Welcome to the past!
KA-POP
Ha ha! It works!!

What a strange era this was! Everything seems so DIFFERENT, so...so NEW.
It looks pretty much like it did when we left, Princess.
Of course it does!

We didn't travel that far through time.
Here, I'll show you how you can use it. Jake, mess up my desk, would you?
Already on it!!

Wow, my desk is all janked up now! Boy, it sure would be great if that never happened!
Ooooh, she's gonna press the button!
Press the button press the button press the button!

Hold on to me, boys.
Oh man! WHEN I FINISH THIS SENTENCE WE WILL BE IN THE

When you finish reading this sentence you will be in the...

See? Now the desk is as good as new!
KA-POP
PAST!
Algebraic to the limit!

Wait. If we're in the past, how come we're not bumping into our past selves?
The machine doesn't work that way, silly!

By shunting the temporal flux through orbitally-opposed capacitors and bypassing the tachyon flow via a magically-inverted antihex we can achieve cross-temporal molecular replacement and anyway **LONG STORY SHORT**, whoever presses the button and whoever's touching **THEM** is sent back in time to replace their previous selves! The time machine takes the place of **ITS** previous self too, which is how come there's not two of them right now.

I understand completely!!

But um, if I had a friend who didn't get it at all, could you explain it again?
What?! I get it, dude!
Just think of it like a do-over button, Finn. If you ever get into a fight and mess up **SO BADLY** you need a do-over, just press this button and you'll be set!

Princess I kinda trashed your lab, and Finn I kinda wrote some brutally honest **AND** embarrassingly flattering verse about you on the walls.

Do-over time!!

...FUTURE!

Jake, I designed this time machine for EMERGENCY USE ONLY. You can't just go nuts and use it all the time! When I did it, it was for DEMONSTRATIONS.
KA-POP
I understand, Princess Gubblebum.

Wait, "Princess Gubblebum"? Ha! Where'd I learn to speak?? I must be crazy!

KA-POP
AHEM. I understand, Princess BUBBLEGUM.

Jake! I'm serious! ONLY USE THE TIME MACHINE IN EMERGENCIES, okay?
Okay, okay, glob! I just ASSUMED you'd prefer to be called by your correct name, Brincess Pugglebum.

Ha ha, my bad! Better RESET THE TIMELIN--
Ow!!

I HEREBY MAKE THE FOLLOWING ROYAL DECREE: messing up my name on purpose isn't reason enough to go back in time, and this applies especially to you, Jake the BOG.
Aw poops.

Be back in a bit, I'm working on my new comic idea, "Jake the Bog and Finn the Shoe-Man"

Aw cabbage, now I'm almost late for the Royal Court! I'll be back in four hours!
Don't press the button while I'm gone, okay?
RRRRRING

Okay. I promise, Princess!
"I" "promise", Princess!
Heh heh heh.

What?
Can't a guy remember a joke he heard earlier, and that's the reason he's laughing, and it's not because he's figured out a way to avoid being trapped by a promise?

I... guess... so?
I've done it!

Anyway, bye!

Okay Jake, **REMEMBER**: we promised we wouldn't press the button unless it was an emergency.
I know, I know. Hey! I've got a great idea!
Let's go out and cause some emergencies, okay buddy?

Um, I don't think that's what she meant.
Oh no! I'm pretty sure it's exactly what she meant!

Looks like we've got a **PAL DISAGREEMENT** brewin', Finn. There's only one way to solve this.
I under-stand, Jake. Let's do this.

BATTLE-HANDS: Rock Paper Scissors!!
In 3...2... 1...

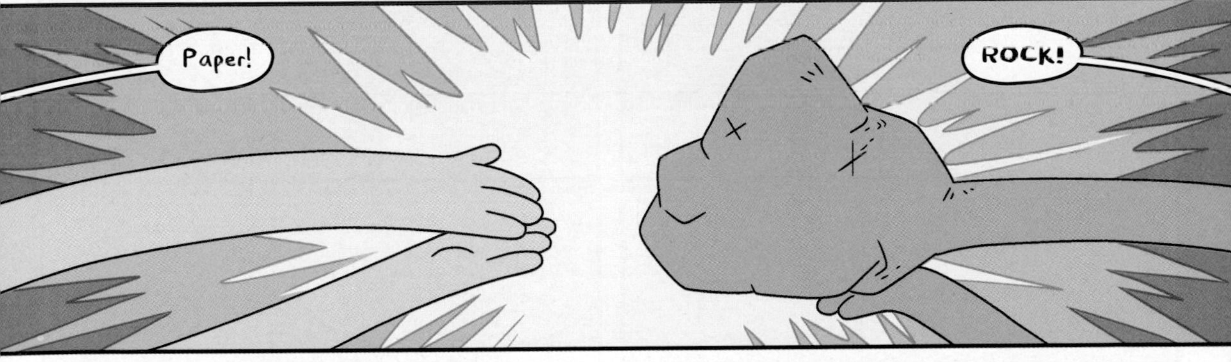
Paper!
ROCK!

Aw man, I lose?! For real?
Sorry dude! Looks like we **DON'T** go out looking for trouble. Looks like we sit here quietly for the next several hours instead!!

Maaaaaaaan.
So... bored...
Wait! Dude, if I press the button without touching you, that means that only I go back in time, right?
I think so. I mean, I'm **PRETTY SURE** that's how it wo--
Perfect!!

I'm back! Finn the Shoe-Man got thrown into Jake the Bog and that's where I ran out of ideas. If you have ideas for what Jake the Bog and Finn the Shoe-Man can do next please let me know.

Dude! Wait, Peebles said that's only for emergencies!
It's an emergency!!
I really really have to win that battle of the hands!

JAKE ARRIVES IN THE PAST:
Jake! I'm serious! ONLY USE THE TIME MACHINE IN EMERGENCIES, okay?
KA-POP
Oh right! Hey you guys!

You were both here the last time we travelled through time, so you're both here now! Only you don't know what happens next because I'm the only one who arrived here from MY future. Okay, that makes sense!
Huh?
Nevermind! Princess, aren't you late for Royal Court?

I don't--
Ah, so I am. Okay. Well, don't press the button while I'm gone unless it's an emergency!
RRRRRING

Okay, okay, later! Finn, let's do Rock Paper Scissors to see if we should go out looking for emergencies!
I-- okay?

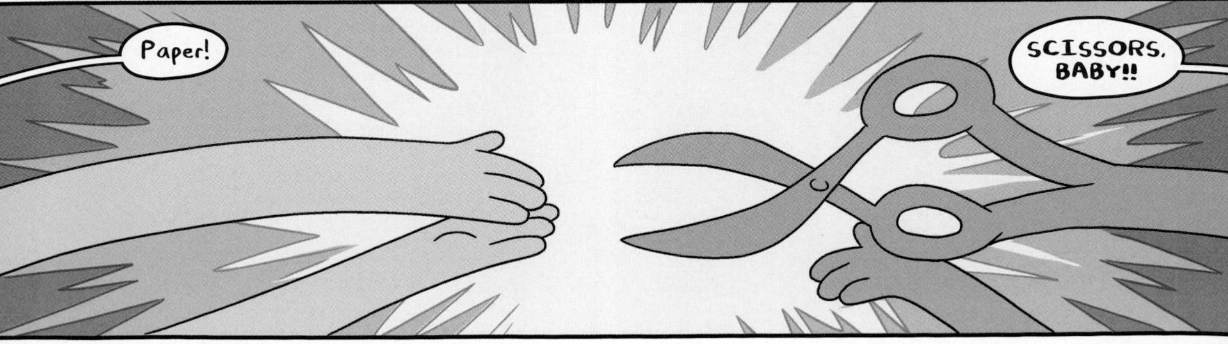
Paper!
SCISSORS, BABY!!

If you don't understand Jake's explanation of time travel then please re-read Jake's explanation of time travel, and he'll explain it for you again!

Dude, I still don't think this is what Princess Bubblegum had in mind!
No man, I'm **PRETTY SURE** sitting around being bored **IS** an emergency. It's a boredom emergency. One that we are now addressing!!

Ow!!
Ow! Ow ow ow!

It's about **TIME** I stopped stubbing my toe!
Huh?

I dunno, man. Puns are hard.

KA-POP
Jake! I'm serious! **ONLY USE THE TIME MACHINE IN EMERGENCIES**, okay?
There! Now I'll be sure not to stub my toe this time!

Huh? Which time?
Princess, you're late for the Royal Court! Emergency button presses only, we got it!

This is the very first instance of someone asking about the time around Finn and Jake where they did not respond with "Adventure Time!" Mark it on your calendars!!

SOON:
Look, I know you still don't think this is what Princess Bubblegum had in mind.
I don't!
But don't worry! We can fix **ANY PROBLEM** now.

See? Look up ahead. There's a bunch of skeletons hanging out. Normally, these skeletons would be a problem, right?
Not really. They're not so tough. Skeletons don't have any muscles, so they fall apart real easy.
EVIL SKELETON FAMILY PICNIC

Hey skeletons! I've got a **BONE** to pick with you!
Oh, "ha ha." Like I've never heard that before.
...Really?

Well, okay! I can be way fresher! Just you wait right here while I go back in time and do things over again!

SOON:
Come on! Hurry up, Finn! This is **SO BORING** the third time around.
It's still new to me, dude!

FINALLY! Hey, skeletons! I have a joke I think you'll find quite... **HUMERUS?**
Huh?
Come on, that's hilarious! The humerus is a bone in the arm! You guys should know this stuff!

Man!
Some days I wonder why I spend so much effort trying to impress strangers!

Me too, man. Me too.

SOON:
KA-POP
Now we'll see who has the REAL funny bone!!

SOON:
KA-POP
This time I'll punch the Ice King BEFORE he throws the iceberg at me!

SOON:
KA-POP
Okay. Right. This time I'll punch the Ice King BEFORE he even picks up the iceberg, so when I punch him the iceberg won't fall on my head.

SOON:
KA-POP
Man, I could totally beat that crossword puzzle way faster the second time!

SOON:
KA-POP
That cake's so nice, I'll eat it twice!!

SOON:
KA-POP
That cake's so nice, I'll eat it THRICE!!

SOON:
KA-POP
I just can't stop eating that cake!!
I think I have a problem.

SOON:
KA-POP
My question is, who would spend a whole day exercising and NOT want to undo it??

SOON:
KA-POP
This time even I don't know why I pressed the button!
Ha! Oh well!!

THAT EVENING:
Hey guys! I'm back from the Royal Court!

Hmm...
NOTHING CRAZY HAPPENED. -JAKE
845

Nothing crazy, huh? Then I'm sure he won't mind if I examine the SECRET BUTTON-PRESS COUNTER I built into the time machine!

SECRET BUTTON PRESS COUNTER
0088121
WHAT?! Eighty-eight thousand presses and then some?!

That means I had to give that stupid royal speech over and over again like 88,121 times and I didn't even realize it!
Diss!

Perhaps time travel really IS too much power to leave in the hands of a 13-year-old boy and his dog.

A fun prank is to leave those "NOTHING CRAZY HAPPENED" notes around even when nothing crazy DID happen. You can't get mad at someone for being factually correct, right??

Oh well, I guess it really was a bad idea after all to mess around with time itself. I now know this time machine must be destroyed!

PRINCESS SMASH!!

Huh. Looks like I got some time on my hands.

Sorry, Princess. I know you want the machine to stay destroyed, but I made a super hard-core mess that I super hard-core don't want to clean up!

I'm pretty sure I can repair this machine.
It'll just take some... time?

PRINCESS SMASH IDEA SOME PEOPLE HAVE THAT PRINCESSES CAN'T SMASH

WHEN WE LAST SAW OUR HEROES, JAKE WAS TRYING TO FIX PRINCESS BUBBLEGUM'S TIME MACHINE!
Fit together, pieces! DON'T YOU LIKE EACH OTHER??

AND FINN HAD GONE TO BED! WE DIDN'T SEE THIS LAST ISSUE, BECAUSE IT'S PRETTY BORING.

SEE? WHAT A SNOREFEST!

PART OF EFFECTIVE NARRATION IS GOING WHERE THE ACTION IS, BUT FINN AND JAKE ARE BEING BORING! SO LET'S SEE WHAT PRINCESS BUBBLEGUM IS UP TO!
Brush your teeth / brush them right / because horrors live in cavities / and they come out at night

MAYBE BMO IS UP TO SOMETHING?
OKAY, THAT IS REALLY INTERESTING, BUT ALSO I'M KINDA CREEPED OUT.

WELL, LET'S JUST WAIT TIL IT'S MORNING! AS THIS COMIC TAKES PLACE IN REAL TIME, PLEASE FALL ASLEEP NOW AND TURN TO THE NEXT PAGE ONLY WHEN IT'S TOMORROW.
Man, I bet this piece isn't THAT important anyway!

Princess Bubblegum's song just came to me, when it was whispered to me in a tiny voice from inside my molars

THE NEXT MORNING:
Finn buddy, wake up!
...come on just five more minutes of sleepy-time...
Finn, it's about adventure!

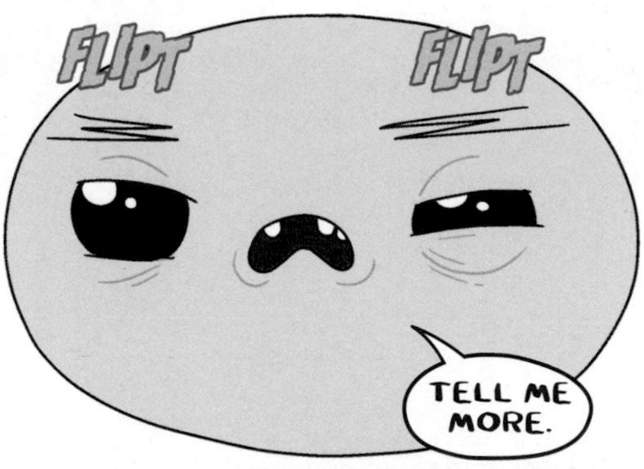
FLIPT
FLIPT
TELL ME MORE.

SOON:
FINN & JAKE
TIMELESS
And since it was night, I snuck over to Princess Bubblegum's lab all creepy-like!
Naturally.

But Princess Bubblegum was already there! She was smashing the time machine, Finn! It took me all night to fix it after she left.
Dude! Not cool!!

If Peebles destroyed the machine she must've had a reason!
And I must've had a reason to fix it too, dude! I thought I had an undo button. I kinda did some things we need to take back!

Look, I'll show you!

Finn is wise, because he knows when porridge is not too hot and not too cold but just right, you want to eat it right away. There are like, whole fairy tales about this one moral.

JAKE'S CRAZY PARTY WHERE YOU CAN DO ANYTHING. I WILL RESET THE TIMELINE, I PROMISE.
NO CUSSING PLEASE! THAT'S RUDE
WOO!
PARTY ALL YOU WANT - I'M A FIX THIS
JAK
BUNS
See? Come on, man.
I promised them a do-over.

Alright, **FINE**. Press the button but **JUST ONCE**, okay? That'll fix all the problems and then we'll destroy the machine for real this time.
That's just the thing, I already tried to fix it but it doesn't do the timey wimey thing anymore! Check it:

TOOT

This? **IS AMAZING**.

TOOT

SOON:
NEPTR! Hey NEPTR! We have a machine we need fixed!
Or maybe we don't! It's kinda math the way it is!
TOOT TOOT TOOOT

It's maybe not be the machine we need...but it is the machine we want.

Hey NEPTR, you're a robot! That means you can fix other robots, right?
TOOTIE TOOT
I will attempt anything the creator wishes me to!! Do you wish it, creator?

Yeah, I guess.
Of course. But an inquiry, creator:

IS THIS MACHINE ALSO DESIGNED TO BE A NEVER-ENDING PIE THROWING ROBOT?

Naw man, it's more of a time travel dealie. It makes toots now though.
Then I would be happy to repair it for you, creator!!

Do you ever worry that he'll get tired of following your orders and try to destroy us all?
Sometimes.
Heh. Yeah.

Are we 100% certain that smashing the machine over and over won't repair it? We are? Okay. But listen: are we 100000000% certain?

SOON:
Here is your machine, creator! I built on what Jake started AND managed to keep the toots!
Schmowza! Thanks NEPTR!

It looks pretty different from before.
Finn, I'm surprised at you. You know it's what's on the INSIDE that counts!

And just like inside each of us, inside of this machine there's a lot of weird parts that I can't fit back together once I take them out.
Come on, let's go!!

KA-TOOT

Aw man, what's this? A giant pile of cardboard boxes?

I don't want to brag, but years of hiding in cardboard boxes has allowed me to write some way realistic cardboard box scenes.

Totally punchable, dude!
Totally had my hands in fists already, dude!

Weird that those boxes were th--
I guess NEPTR didn't quite get the machine ri--

Jake, your face has this really cool scar that makes you look awesome tough!!
Finn, you're a SUPER-RIPPED adult now!!
Ha, seriously?

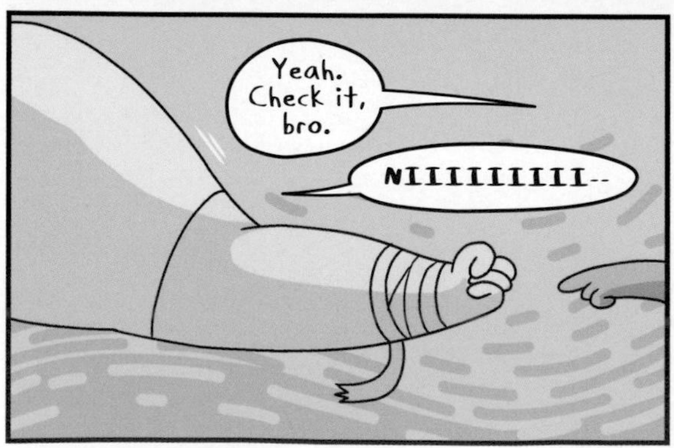
Yeah. Check it, bro.
NIIIIIIIII--

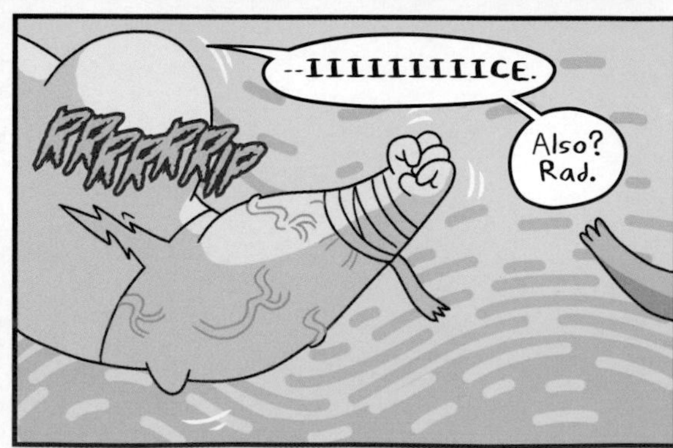
--IIIIIIIIICE.
Also? Rad.

If you start now, you too can grow up into a super-ripped adult, even if you're a super-ripped adult already! You just keep getting more and more ripped until it's kinda awkward actually

Jake, let's get BMO to press the button! I wanna see how ripped a computer can get!
BUMP!
Oh man oh man oh man!

BMO, check out our sweet new bods that we got for free!
Press the dang button, BMO!!

...BMO?
Hey, how come everything looks so old and busted?

Well I for one do NOT remember leaving the kitchen this dirty.
Jake, I think the time machine is janked. It made our bodies awesome, but it also messed up the house.

Okay Jake, ACTION PLAN: we go find PB, you admit that you messed with her machine, and we ask her to fix everything.
Aw man! FINE.

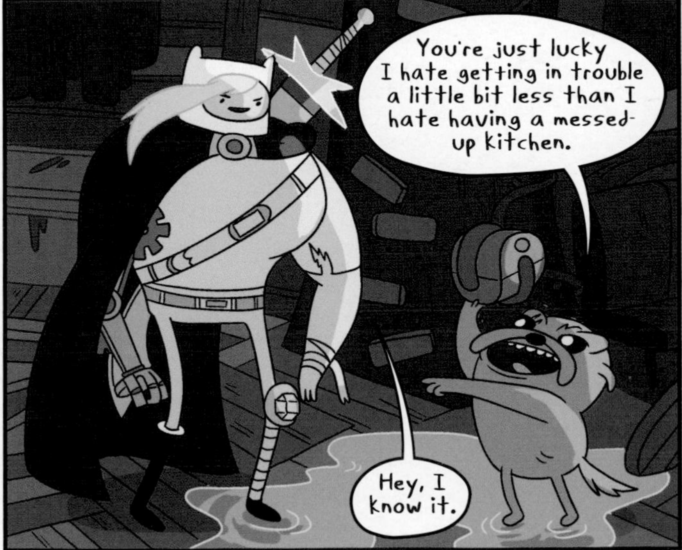
You're just lucky I hate getting in trouble a little bit less than I hate having a messed-up kitchen.
Hey, I know it.

"FINN & JAKE / TIMELESS" clock? See how well it fits into this story? Did I TRULY go back in time to make sure that this clock would already be shown in the cartoon years in the past, just to set it up for this comic? I'LL NEVER SAY.

Ready, buddy?
Ready!

Then here we goooooo ooo--

--OOOOO!
Whoa, dude! You're a big gross hairy spider!
Ha! What?

BUMP!
SWEET! I didn't even do it on purpose. It's like my body WANTED to do it!
Man, you GOTTA follow wherever your body takes you!

BEHIND THE SCENES: the script for this page reads "Jake is now a giant spider, and it's awesome but also kinda gross." This is because I wanted to remind the artists that spiders are awesome, but also, kinda gross!

Hey Finn, I think I can make a web come out my butt!
In a sec. Dude, does everything seem, like--different to you?

Yeah, it looks like someone smashed up all their...cool machines?
Glob. What'd that button **DO?**

WHOAH!
OW!

Jake! We're getting lazered by a robot!!
I know! It's way awesome but it really hurts too!

This is for shooting me in the walkin' sticks!!
Rest in pieces!!
LIGHT AMPLIFICATION BY ZETA-WAVE EMISSION RECOVERY

LAZER beams are better than LASER beams. Ask any scientist!!

Jake, does he look like a robot me to you?
Man, it's like looking into a robot mirror, only you're the dude standing in front of the mirror!!

I, um--
I-I-I-I-
I think we should go see Princess Bubblegum now.

SOON:
Princess Bubblegum! It's Finn and Jake!
We got awesomer!!

Hello?
Finn! Is that you?

What's up?!

AAAHHHHHHH!
You guys are so silly! Like you've never seen me with my Science Robot Welding Mask on before!!

Princess, I--
"Princess"? I haven't been called that in a long time, Finn. It's Queen Bubblegum now. You guys know that!
We do?

Wait a second. What's the last non-messed up thing you remember, Finn?
We pressed the button on your time machine that we tried to fix!
And then our bods got rad but every-thing else got wack!

Oh my goodness! This is just as I feared: the machine sent a temporal duplicate of your minds into your future bodies!! You don't remember the past 15 years, do you?
Man, I don't even remember what I had for breakfast.

But you were also left in the present, where you lived out the past one and a half decades. Only now those memories have been overwritten by the minds you sent forward 15 years ago, so you don't remember them anymore!
Wait. We're in the future?
It's 15 years after the day you pressed the button!

That does explain why I have this rockin' manbod, but still love youth culture!
So!
...What'd we miss?

Wait. I mean, what'd we miss ***BESIDES*** tons of episodes of all our favorite shows??

From my point of view, after you pressed the button, you came to me and explained the time machine didn't work anymore. I was mad that you tried to repair it in the first place, but-- well, I can't stay mad at you guys.
The next day, BMO presented the Finn and Jake robots it'd been building for weeks that you totally never noticed. All seemed awesome at first...
We fought them off that night, forcing them to retreat into the woods. But the next day, they came back.
Overnight, they'd figured out how to build more of themselves. And these ones started out heckuva evil. They didn't even have to wait for it to rain!
We spent years fighting them with all the magic we had, but how do you defeat an enemy that replenishes itself every night? We tried.
We failed.
But over the years, we learnt from them.

...and you had them do all your chores while you went out and adventured all the time.
But we didn't realize their fatal flaw! There was a bug in their programming or something, because as soon as they got wet, these robots turned **HECKUVA EVIL**.
The robots renamed themselves from "F1NN" and "J4KE" to "TERM N8R" and "KILL-O-TRON". At first we thought it was cute! Then they started trying to terminate us!!
You barely made it out alive.
We duplicated their lazers. We upgraded ourselves. I got my Science Hand, Finn got a neato arm and Jake started changing into more powerful forms. We can destroy individual robots more easily now, but they're still a huge threat in numbers. We must remain...vigilant.
NEPTR still helps us fight, but even in the future pies are still pretty useless against robots. And BMO? Well, nobody's seen BMO since the robots first returned that morning fifteen years ago.
BMO

And that brings you up to speed. Sorry for narrating so much!
S'cool.

I promise you, Peebles, that Jake and I will--
It's Queebles now, Finn. Queen Bubblegum, remember? "Queebles."

I promise you, Queebles, that Jake and I will help you defeat these evil robots!!
Yeah, those robots made an error when they messed with our friends! A **FATAL ERROR**.

I appreciate that, Finn, but that's what you've been doing for the past 15 years and all we've managed is a stalemate. You've been fighting all this time too, remember! But those memories got replaced.
Oh. Right.
No biggie though! I've got a better idea!

Mahhe heu han hiix hiss hoim mahhine hinsteaa?

I **SAID**, maybe you can fix this time machine instead?
Yes! Then we can go back in time and prevent this from happening in the first place!!

ACTUAL WRITING TIP: to write a character talking with something in their mouth, just put your own fist in your mouth and write down the sounds you make. I--kinda like writing alone.

Unfortunately, the three of us have been trying THAT for the past fifteen years too. Check out these rad time machines we made. Pretty sweet, right?

Unfortunately, none of them work. Near as I can tell, your time machine was powered by some magic that only existed during those first few days, and we're too far away from it now. Go ahead, press the button on your machine. You won't go anywhere.

Huh. Those toots are pretty neat though.
I know, right?
TOOT

I'm sorry, Finn and Jake, but I can't send you back OR forward in time. I'm afraid you're both stuck here in this crazy, nutty future...
Don't say forever don't say forever don't say forever

...FOREVER!!
AW BARFS.

"Come on, Finn, the future's not THAT terrible! Look on the bright side: evil robots haven't attacked for like, LITERALLY days!"

KNOCK
KNOCK
Who is it?
UH...GOOD ROBOTS

Nice!
No, Jake, wait!
We don't **HAVE** any good robots, Jake!!

Ow, you guys!!
What about **NEPTR?**
He's more of a cyborg now.

OW AGAIN, YOU GUYS!
Jake! Can you give me fifteen seconds?!

I dunno. I mean, probably?
I'm pretty sure there's not much I'm bad at??

If you're just starting with this chapter, then the backstory you need to know is two things: **IT'S THE FUTURE** and **EVIL ROBOTS ARE ATTACKING.** Okay! Let's go! These robots aren't going to beat up themselves! *Nobody programmed them to do that!!*

Hey! Robots!

I've got something PRESSING to tell you!!

Don't be jerks!!
ALSO, IT'S FUNNY THAT I SAID "PRESSING" BECAUSE I'M GOING TO SMUSH YOU!

I DON'T KNOW IF YOU WERE PROGRAMMED TO GET JOKES OR WHAT.

Quick, Finn! Jake can't hold them off for long!
Okay! I'll be quick!!
...to do what?

To arm yourself! Grab something amazing!
Whoa! I don't know which cyborg dealie I want first!!

— No, wait!!

You guys, I hope you're ready because I guess there IS a limit on how often I can get lazered in the face!!

I'm sorry Finn! I'm sorry Bubblegum! I can't hold them back any longer!!

Um... howdy?

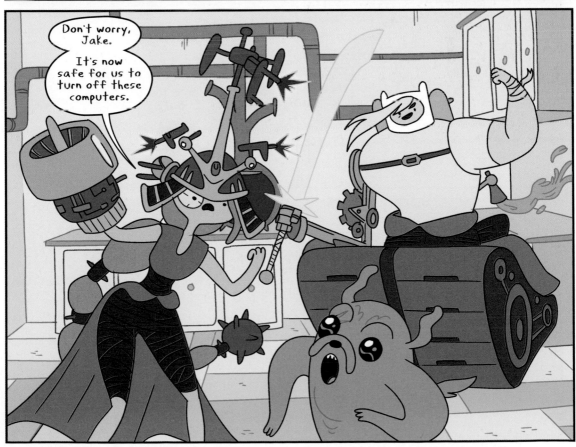

Don't worry, Jake.

It's now safe for us to turn off these computers.

May I present... Battlemode Bubblegum and Tank Adventure Finn With Borrowed Tank Dress That Doesn't Come Off.

Dude! Stick something awesome on your arms!
Ha ha! Okay!

How come you don't wear these tank treads all the time, Bubblegum?
What?
Cuz they get all sweaty and gross!!

Finn, there's not just cool weapons back there! There's also hats!!

Oh man! Grab one for me too?
This isn't dress-up, guys! Focus on destroying these robots!!

FINE.

If you looked at my search history you would find "Jake in a fedora," "does Jake look cool in a fedora," "I want to see Jake in a fedora" and "what if Jake had extra arms and a fedora, is that illegal??"

So um, those guns only had one shot each. It's a design failure, I know.
How many of these robots **ARE** there?!
I'll find out!

Aw man! This whole place is globbed up to the ultimate max!!

Guys, I think we're pooched!
NO WE'RE NOT! Jake, give me a bubble shield! Finn, ditch the jetpack and tank legs!
But I love my tank legs!

Come on, Finn!
Tank legs, you make me feel like I've woken up after a lifetime of slumber! I'll never forget you, tank legs!!

Man. Regular legs are insanely boring!
Yeah, but they don't blow up like tank legs do. Five seconds, Jake!
Got it!

BEEP BEEP BEEP BEEP BEEP

BEEP BEEP BEEP BEEP

BEEP BEEP BEEP
Butts to meet you!

Jake, get us out of here!!
BEEP BEEP

Okay! Nobody sneeze in there!
Every time I imagine someone sneezing inside me I get all grossed out!
BEEEEEEEEEP

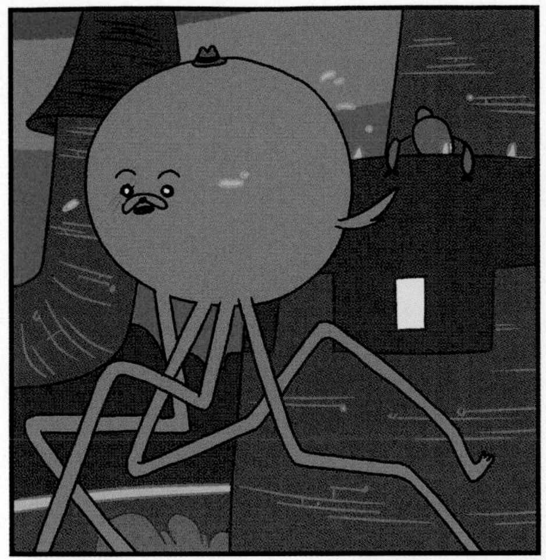

KABOOM

That's it. We've lost the Candy Kingdom.

Don't be sad, Bubblegum! We'll... we'll fight them! We'll take it back!
It's too late, Finn. There's nothing we can do.

Ouch! Watch it, Jake! I'm not made of bruises, I'm made of **BUBBLEGUM**, remember?
It's **KINDA** in my name.

Choose Goose's
WEAPONS & JUICES
Guys! Look who I ran into!
CHOOSE GOOSE!!

You may be thinking of Bruise Princess, who both delivers, and is made of, bruises

Who should be here but Candy Royalty, and two strapping men of sworn candy loyalty?
Hey Choose Goose. I'm from the past now!
Me too!!

Choose Goose, the Candy Kingdom has fallen. We need more weapons. Do you have anything you can sell us?
Here's something that'll strike a chord: a giant lazer-powered ultimate sword!

How much?
Though I also want to end this robot dystopia, to trade at a loss would show awful myopia!
What're you saying there, Choosie Goosie?

It means he's not going to give it to us for cheap.
CG, there's killer robots we need to beat! **AND** beat up!
One leads to the other!
Killer robots I condemn, but I shan't part with this sword for less than fifty red gems!

Hmmm...looks like all I've got is forty-nine red gems. Is that okay?
ABSOLUTELY NOT! And you'd better run, because you're about to get caught!

Aw man. Jake, we'll need an army to hold them off!
Finn! I just had a really blooby idea!
Tops blooby?
YOU TELL ME.

Sir, if I may be so bold as to inquire: precisely how blooby are we talking about here??

Check me out, dude! Check out how awesome I made my fingers!
And look at the awesome fingers on THOSE guys!
We scale this up and we get...
FRACTAL GLOB JAKE!!
WHAAAAAT!!
Total tops blooby has been achieved!

Come on, Finn! That'll only buy us a few minutes at best.
He's done that before?

He does it all the time!
Whoa.
The future is **AWESOME.**

Jake! Meet us at Marceline's Cave!
Yep!

SOON:
Guys I punched the robots for as long as I could! I think they're about five minutes behind me!
I'll take it. This door should hold them for another five.

Whoa! What happened here?
Marceline-- she...she...

...I don't want to talk about it.

What?! Is she... **DEAD??**
She's a vampire, Finn. So...yes? She's undead?
...Like always?

She just doesn't live here anymore, dudes.
PHEW

But **WE'RE** stuck here, and we've only got ten minutes left until those robots reach us, and we've got nowhere left to run. I'm, uh...
...open to suggestions?
This may sound like cheating, but, well--why don't we just invent a machine to send us back in time so we can prevent this from happening in the first place?

Finn, I'd love to, but it's like I said: we've been trying to get time machines to work for years, and we haven't had any luck.
Yeah, but that's the thing! **YOU'VE** been trying to get them to work. Why should you have to do all the work? Maybe you'll figure it out 30 years from now!

Let Future Me and Future You and Future Jake do the heavy lifting!! They've got all the time in the world!
I never thought of it that way, actually! It's worth a try, right?

The maneuver Finn has invented here will be henceforth known as the "Deus Ex Tempus," which is Latin for "Whoa this is TOTALLY AWESOME!!"

JAKE, BUBBLEGUM: I SWEAR WE'LL ESCAPE FROM HERE AND I'LL SPEND THE REST OF MY DAYS WORKING ON A TIME MACHINE.
BUBBLEGUM, FINN: I WILL DO THE SAME AND WHEN WE INVENT IT WE'LL TOTALLY SEND IT BACK IN TIME TO THIS VERY MOMENT TO SAVE US ALL!
DUDES, TOGETHER THE THREE OF US WILL BE UNSTOPPABLE!

Jake, did you REALLY mean what you said?
Dude! You know how hard it's gonna be to invent a time machine from scratch?
This is a LOT of WORK we're talking about!

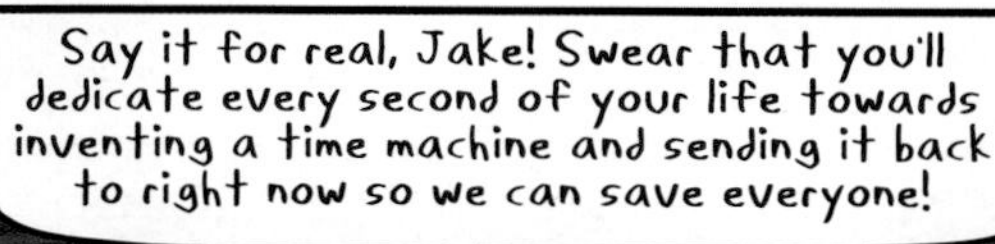
Say it for real, Jake! Swear that you'll dedicate every second of your life towards inventing a time machine and sending it back to right now so we can save everyone!

FINE, FINE. I promise I'll do that thingy you said or whatever!

Come on, Jake!
I HEREBY SWEAR TO TURN ALL MY MAGICAL POWERS TOWARDS MAKING THIS DREAM OF A KICKING SWEET TIME MACHINE A REALITY!!!
Say it like you mean it!!
I'M SAYING THIS FOR REAL THIS TIME TOO!

WE ARE DOING THIS, BROS!!
WE ARE MAKING THIS HAPPEN!!

Ha Ha! NICE.
But there's only two seats!
Wait, there's a note there from our future selves!

OKAY SO HERE IT IS OR WHATEVER! QB SAYS SHE SHOULD STAY BEHIND. I'M WRITING THAT, QB! I JUST WROTE THAT. ANYWAY DUDES USE THIS MACHINE WELL BECAUSE IT WAS A LOT OF WORK AND IT KINDA SUCKED TO HAVE TO WORK SO HARD.
-FUTURE OLD MAN JAKE

Future Old Man Jake is right. You two should go. My place--my time--is here. I'll be fine.
Go fix this, Finn. Fix the world.

You--I thought--
I mean, we...
Finn, six years is a big age difference when you're eighteen. But when you get older...
...it's not that big a deal.

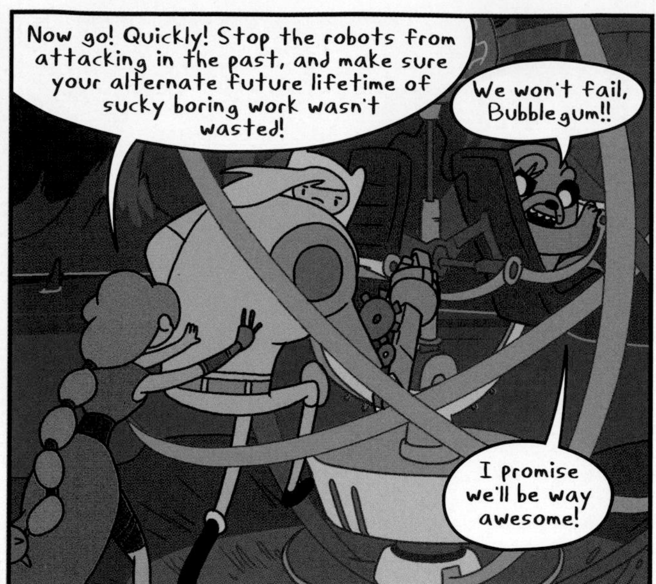
Now go! Quickly! Stop the robots from attacking in the past, and make sure your alternate future lifetime of sucky boring work wasn't wasted!
We won't fail, Bubblegum!!
I promise we'll be way awesome!

KRA-KOW

DID YOU KNOW: Sucky boring work is so flippin' sucky and boring

Bubblegum! It's me, BMO! I'm back! It took years, but I finally came up with a way to beat the evil robots!
BMO

All we need are giant robot suits!!

BMO, this is amazing! But Finn and Jake just went back in time to stop all this from happening, so um...
...we're good?

Oh.
BMO

Neat! Well, until they do that, want to beat up those bad guys?
Um, obvs!!
BMO

BMO

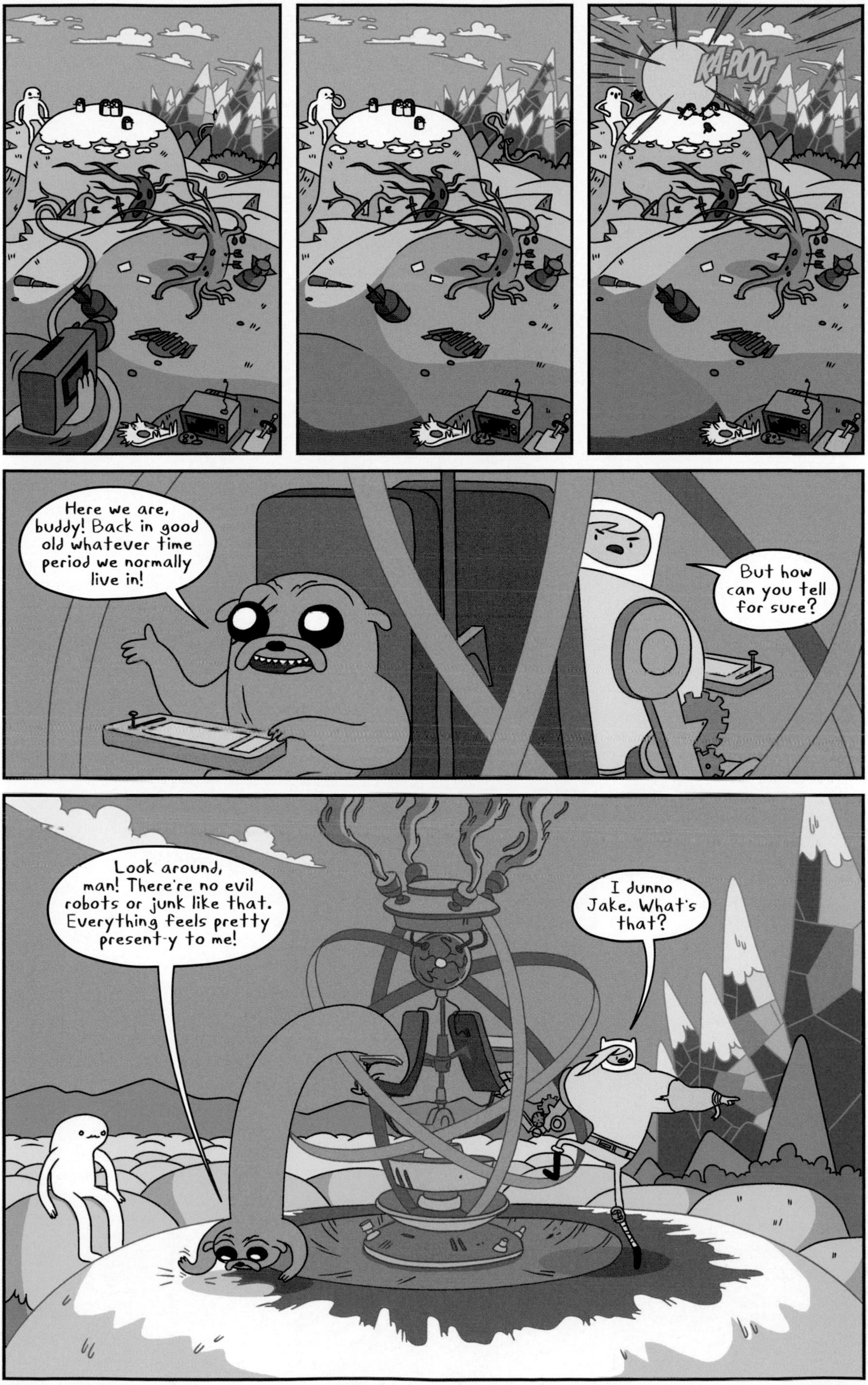

KA-POOT

Here we are, buddy! Back in good old whatever time period we normally live in!
But how can you tell for sure?

Look around, man! There're no evil robots or junk like that. Everything feels pretty present-y to me!

I dunno Jake. What's that?

ADVENTURE TIME, ISSUE 1:
The Land of Ooo: A pretty magical place! Jake and Finn live here. Adventure possibility: UNLIMITED??
Ice King: All he wants to do is marry a princess, and he thinks stealing them is okay!
Jake the Dog: Magical dog with stretchy powers. Pal rating at 110%!
Finn the Human: Awesome dude with awesome hat. Pal rating at 110%!
Really good at being pals AND at adventures!
The Lich: HE IS COMING.
Aww, dude! We went too far back in time! We did that junk over there like EIGHT MONTHS ago!!
Princess Bubblegum: Human/bubblegum ruler of the Candy Kingdom. She's made of gum! She and Finn are friends, and sometimes feelings can get complicated, you know?
Not as important as the other boxes, just a heads up.
Written by Ryan North
Art by Shelli Paroline
and Braden Lamb
"Adventure Time" created by
Marceline the Vampire Queen: Over a thousand years old. Be cool, okay?
Heh. Memories.
BMO runs on electricity and likes taking nice pictures
who is currently sitting in a chair in

2 TRIP(S) REMAINING
Don't worry, Finn. We'll just hop into the time machine and go forward in time a little bit! It says it's still got two trips left, so we're good.
Sweet!
Oh my GLOB, stop moving you guys! I wanna take another one, and you're ruining my lumpin' photo!!

Ready, buddy?
Ready!
TIME TRAVEL ADVENTURE TIME!!

..travel adventure time travel adventure time travel adventure time...

ADVENTURE TIME, ORIGINAL PILOT EPISODE:
ZZZ

ZZZ
KA-POOT

Oh no. Oh *YES*.

ZZZ

Jake, you went back even further!! This is **YEARS** ago. This is back when I loved pens **SO MUCH** that I made everyone call me "Pen"!

I'm sorry man! Nobody ever trained me how to do time travel junk!! I just press whatever buttons feel right, you know?

Hey look, I'm out of bed now! And I'm dancing! **NICE!**
And look, it's your old sleeping bag! **DOUBLE NICE!**

How come you never told me my dance moves are **AMAZINGLY SWEET?!?**
Hey man, I thought you knew!

Okay, well, past us's have this well in hand. Let's peel out, Jake! **TO THE MAX!**
Also, I'm driving this time.
I hate to see me go, but I love to watch me leave!

Look! It's Princess Bubblegum's Rainicorn! She looked like she was crying.
Hey, I remember this! Oh man! Those other us's are gonna cheer up Lady Rainicorn **SO HARD!**
Well let's go cheer her up! **TO THE MAX!**

Stop reading this comic, go watch the original pilot episode, and notice that Finn's sleeping bag really does disappear!
YES. THIS IS ACTUALLY HAPPENING. THIS IS REAL LIFE, AND THERE'S NO GOING BACK.

Wait, Jake, we can't take this with us! We've got to put it back or we'll mess up our own histories! Our own **SLEEP** histories, dude!!
But this is when you lost it in the first place, remember?

Oh yeah!! Wow. I kinda wondered what happened to this bad boy!
Wait, hold on! That means there's something I have to do!

There. Perfect.

All done, buddy?
All done! Time travel's not so hard, Jake. You need to remember one rule: like in all things, you've just got to be kind.

You know, it's funny: I always wondered who gave me that rad advice!
KA-POOT

Hey, Pen! Pens are math (we all know it) but using your real name is like, math times five!! Love you forever, me.
P.S. I borrowed your sleeping bag

ADVENTURE TIME, ISSUE 5:
Finally some time alone! Now I can continue building my CREEPY FINN AND JAKE ROBOTS.

KA-POOT
Yay! This looks more like it! Let's go ask BMO what time period we're in!
And then let's sleep inside this bag!!

BMO! BMO! What time is it?

Finn! Jake! I calculate it to be ADVENTURE TIME within a margin of error of 5%, 19 times out of 20!
What are you guys doing home so early?

Whoa!! When did you guys upgrade your cases?!
I wanna upgrade my case too!
GOOD AT THIS

BMO, we're from the future! Our bods are, anyway. Our brains are from around this time though!
But where'd you get the time machine?
From the future!

Of course!
All the best stuff is there!!

BMO just dropped an ERROR 15623: BOD/MEMORY OF BOD MISMATCH

Listen, BMO, we know about the surprise you've been working on for us.
Aw! You do?!
Yep! Robot Jake and Robot Finn! They're kinda amazing, BMO!
i hope i'm GOOD AT THIS

...and then you'd have more time, for maybe...
...for maybe playing with BMO?
i hope i'm GOOD AT THIS

And it's super sweet that you've been doing this for us! You're the best.

I wanted them to do your chores for you! That way you'd have more time for adventures! And--and...

BMO, real talk: if I could play video games all day long, I would. I would literally sit and never move and play games until forever. I'd put up a Do Not Disturb sign that read "PLAYING VIDEO GAMES FOREVER NOW, HA HA HA SWEEEEET"
Yaaaaay!

But here's the thing, BMO: if those robots get wet, they'll turn evil and build more of themselves and eventually they'll destroy everything! That's what we travelled back in time to prevent!
OH SNAP!!

Well! What are we waiting for, gentlemen?
Let's punch the bad robots until they're broken!!

In a cut scene from the previous chapter, Finn and Jake were hiding from the evil robots, and Jake made his time machine toot, and one evil robot turned to the other and said "Hey, are you dropping bad packets in here?" It was extremely hilarious.

SOON:
Dude. We just saved Queen Bubblegum AND the entire Future Candy Kingdom AND killed our robot selves!
GO US!!

But wait: if you stopped your reason for travelling back in time, how come you still travelled back in time? Shouldn't you have disappeared or whatever? And how come you still remember the future if that didn't happen anymore?

Who knows, BMO! I guess time travel is just TOTALLY CRAY?
Cray to the zee, baby!!

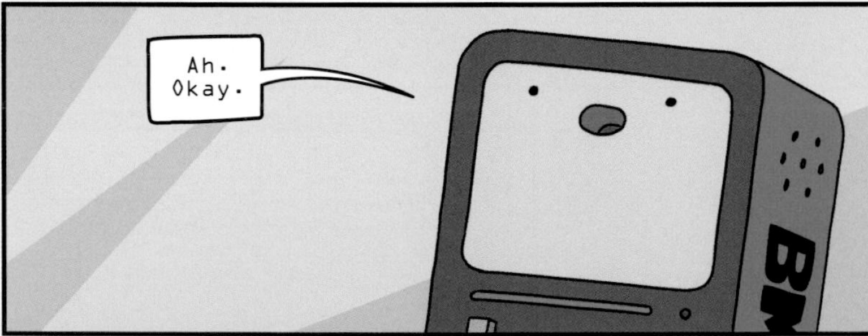
Ah. Okay.

So!
Those older bods mean you'll get to be wimpy old men way way sooner now, right?

TRUE FACTS: Cray to the zee, or cray^zee, is how you spell "crazy" in a cray^zee way

AAHHHHH! I don't want to be a senior yet!
AAAAHHHHHH!! I DON'T WANT TO BE A SENIOR EVER!!

There's only one person who can help us now...
I hear you, bro. Let's go see--

PRINCESS BUBBLEGUM!!
DR. PRINCESS!!

Oh. Dr. Princess could help us too, I guess. She IS a medical doctor.
Huh.
No man, it's cool. She can be our backup, in case Princess Bubblegum toots out on us.

SOON:
Princess Bubblegum! Guess who brought the party to you!
It's us! We brought the party!!

By reading this page carefully you can determine that, yes, Finn and Jake ran most of the way to Princess Bubblegum's castle, then ran all the way back to their house because they forgot to bring the time machine, then ran all the way there again. Physical fitness! It's worth it!

Finn! Jake! What happened to your bods?!
We're from the future, that's what! But we have the minds of our regular selves.
Man, we totally just explained this to **BMO**!!

Listen, we fixed the future so you won't get attacked anymore by the evil robot versions of us that destroyed the Candy Kingdom--
Attacked? **DESTROYED?!**
No, listen, I said we fixed it!!

But now we're stuck in these crazy bods which, while awesome, also means we'll be too old too soon, Princess!
We'll be old dudes, Peebles!
I'm already, like, 28!!

Well, can't you use your time machine to fix that?
Nope! This one's used up, plus it doesn't change our bods. We used a different one for that. We left it in the future though.
We're not super good at this!!

Please? Can't you, like, smush your time machine into this one? And then, like...pour some science on it?
PLEASE, Princess? **PLEASE** will you drop some science all over our business??
Finn, Jake, I'm sorry, but science simply doesn't work that way.

Just kidding, guys!
Science totally works that way!!

My question: why would you even *STUDY* science if you're not going to pour it on stuff??

SHORTLY:
Stand back, boys. It's possible this semiliquid science might react with the temporal particle discharger and destroy the entire space-time contin--
DING

Success!! Wow. I'd worry about the consequences and side-effects of using this machine, but you guys seem pretty into this so...I don't know, give it a try!
Young bods, here we come!!
Yay!

Whatever happens when you press that button, Finn and Jake, know this: that was a really kickin' science experiment. I'd been looking for something to pour that on for a while. See you soon!
See you sooner, P-bubs!

Ha, wait, I almost forgot! Hey Princess! You and Finn totally smooched in the future!!

What? You smooched!!
We all saw it.

Aw, Jake!!
What? I was right there, man.

Brother, you know you gotta do that tier two stuff behind a hill or a sheet or whatever if you don't want me to know about it!

ZZZZZZT

It worked! We're young again!
Ha ha! It's all I ever wanted and more!!

This looks like--outside PB's Sciencetorium? And the door's fixed and everything?
Weiiiiird.

Hey Princess! It worked!
Check out our awesome bods!

Yes, yes, you both have awesome bods.
What's going on, Princess?
I'm sorry; I'm a bit distracted. The time machine I was just about to finish inventing totally just... disappeared! It was here one second, then there was a nutty intense burst of rainbow light, and it's gone.

Hey, come to think of it, our time machine's gone too!

Wait. You guys had a time machine?
Dude, that machine we cobbled together must've not JUST been a time machine. It was a time machine that also erased all the other time machines! So the whole thing never happened and we got our bods back!!
Of course! That was one incredible machine!

Totally confused over here, boys.
But we got to keep our memories of it, and now we know how to make sure the future will turn out fine! No evil robots now!!
Also we got a new bag souvenir to sleep in!

There were evil robots...in the future?
Not anymore!!

RRRRRING
Aw cabbage, now I'm almost late for the Royal Court! I'll come by later, and we can talk more about...whatever this is... then, okay?
Okay!
Do what you gotta do, Princess!

Man, it's too bad nobody remembers our adventure but us.
No it's not! That means we've got a secret, Finn! And you know what secrets are?

Secrets are the glue that sticks friends together!
Exactly! And we've got a big one! So that means...
BEST FRIENDS FOREVER!!

FIRST BANK OF OOO

I'd like to withdraw this in 15 years, please! It's for a neato sword.

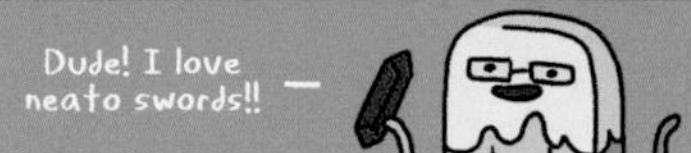
Dude! I love neato swords!!

Hey BMO!
We're back from Princess Bubblegum's place!
BMO, you around?
Wait. The robots are back together!

I guess we never smashed them up in this timeline after all, since the time machine never got invented? Man. We **ARE** kinda sucky at time travel.
Hey man, whatever, who cares? You go tell BMO what's up, and I'll smash these robots again!

AND SO...
So yeah, that's why we have to destroy your presents, even if they are **WAY TOTALLY AWESOME** before they turn evil and try to kill everyone.
S'cool, Finn. I get it!
Man, programming things so they don't turn evil is HARD.

So. What do you wanna do now?
What would you do if I said I want to play...
...video games?

:D
BMO

Ask any programmer: making sure your programs won't turn evil is totes the hardest part.

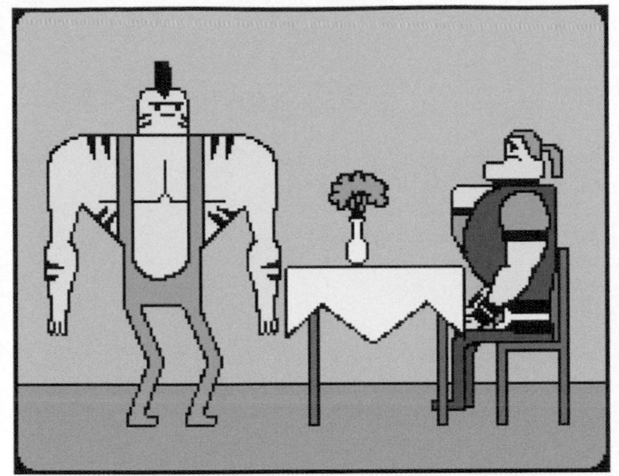

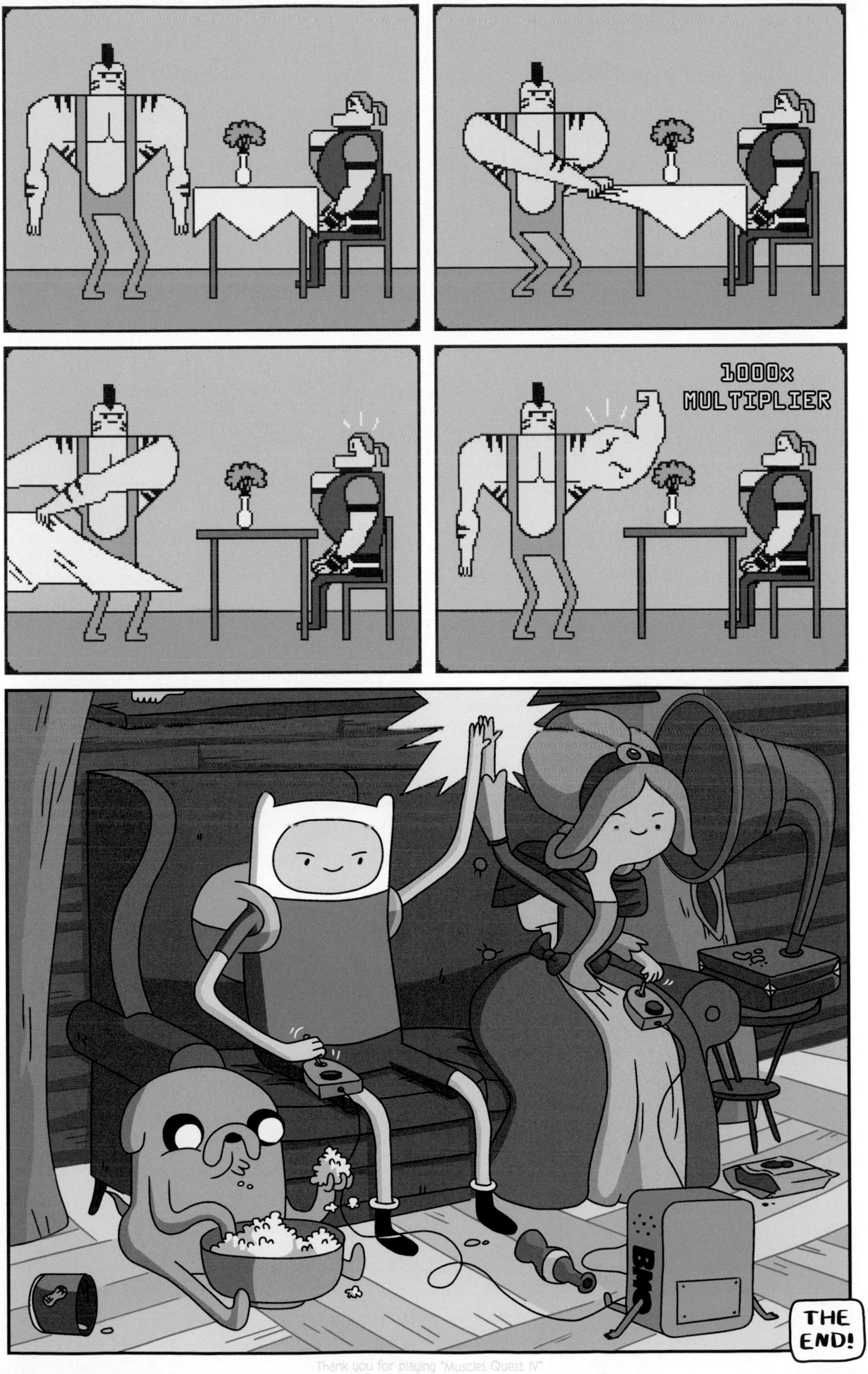

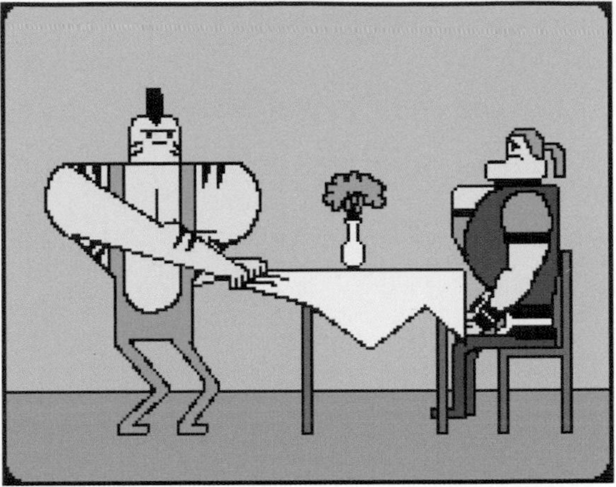

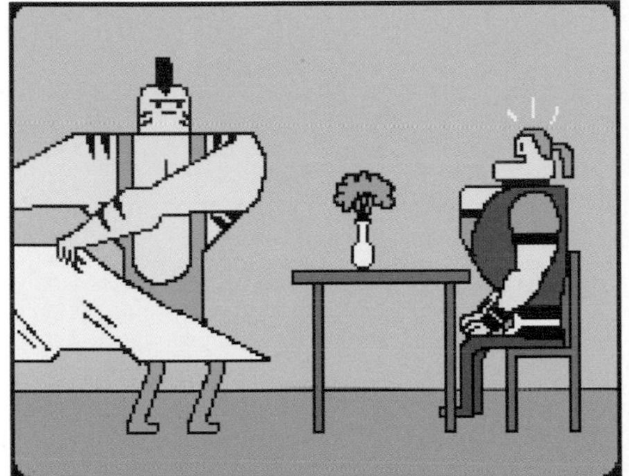

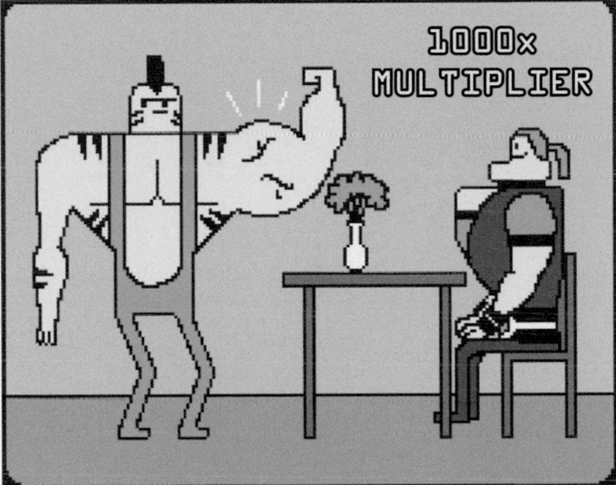
1000x
MULTIPLIER

BMO

THE END!

Thank you for playing "Muscles Quest IV"

COVER GALLERY

BMO
CHRIS HOUGHTON

Cover 5A:
Chris Houghton
Colors: Kassandra Heller

Cover 5B:
Eleanor Davis

KOCHALKA
Cover 5C:
James Kochalka

Cover 5D:
Mike "Gabe" Krahulik
BMO

CHRIS HOUGHTON

Cover 6A:
Chris Houghton
Colors: Kassandra Heller

Cover 6B:
James Lloyd
J.LLOYD '12

JAKE

Cover 6C:
Dan Hipp

Cover 6D:
Steve Wolfhard

CHRIS
HOUGHTON

Cover 7A:
Chris Houghton
Colors: Kassandra Heller

Cover 7B:
Jason Ho

Cover 7C:
Graham Annable

-GRAHAM-

Cover 7D:
Franco

Cover 8A:
Chris Houghton
Colors: Kassandra Heller
CHRIS HOUGHTON

SAND
ND
SAND
drew weing '12

Cover 8B:
Drew Weing

BMO
BM
COOVER

Cover 8C:
Colleen Coover

Cover 8D:
Phil McAndrew

CHRIS HOUGHTON

Cover 9A:
Chris Houghton
Colors: Kassandra Heller

Cover 9B:
Shannon Wheeler

WHEELER

ADVENTURE TIME
BMO
JQ2012

Cover 9C:
Joe Quinones

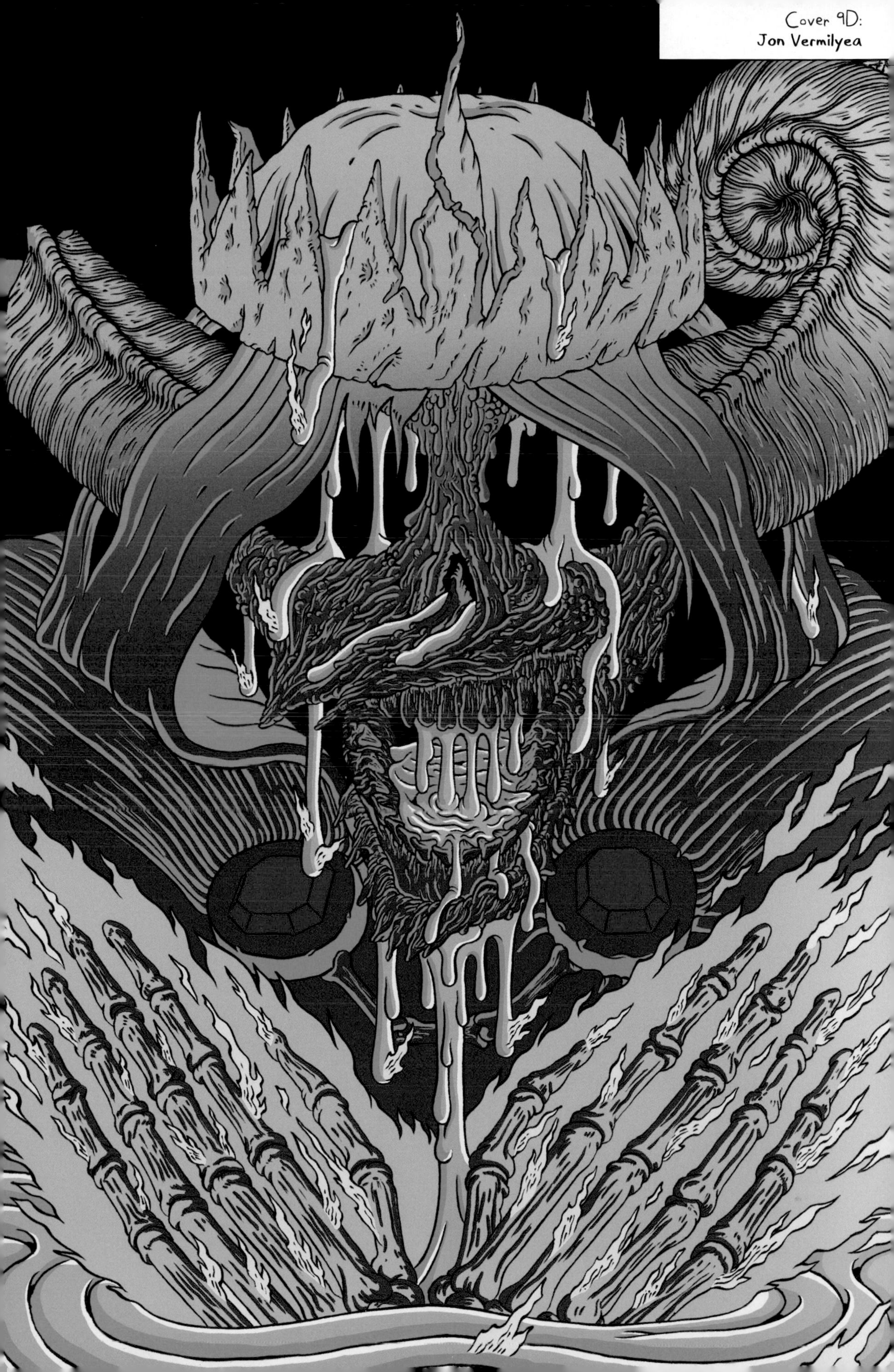

Cover 9D:
Jon Vermilyea